P9-DCY-467

For Elaine

and

my family in Moscow

Illustrations copyright © 1993 by Olga Zharkova.

First published in 1993 by ABC, All Books for Children,
a division of The All Children's Company Ltd.,
33 Museum Street, London WC1A 1LD, England.
All rights reserved. Published by Scholastic Inc.,
730 Broadway, New York, NY 10003, by arrangement with
All Books For Children, a division of The All Children's Company, Ltd.
SCHOLASTIC HARDCOVER ® is a registered trademark of Scholastic Inc.

No part of this publication may be reproduced in whole or in part, or stored in a retrieval system,
or transmitted in any form or by any means, electronic, mechanical, photocopying, recording, or otherwise,
without written permission of the publisher. For information regarding permission, write to
All Books for Children, a division of The All Children's Company, Ltd.,
33 Museum Street, London WC1A 1LD, England.

Library of Congress Cataloging-in-Publication Data
We three kings / illustrated by Olga Zharkova
p   cm.
Summary: An illustrated edition of the traditional Christmas song.
ISBN 0-590-46433-7
1. Carols—Texts. 2. Christmas music. [1. Carols. 2. Christmas music.] I. Zharkova, Olga. ill.
PZ8.3.W367 1993
782.28' 1723—dc20   92-38571
                                                                  CIP
                                                                  AC

12 11 10 9 8 7 6 5 4 3 2 1   3 4 5 6 7 8/9
Printed in Singapore
First Scholastic printing, October 1993

WE THREE KINGS

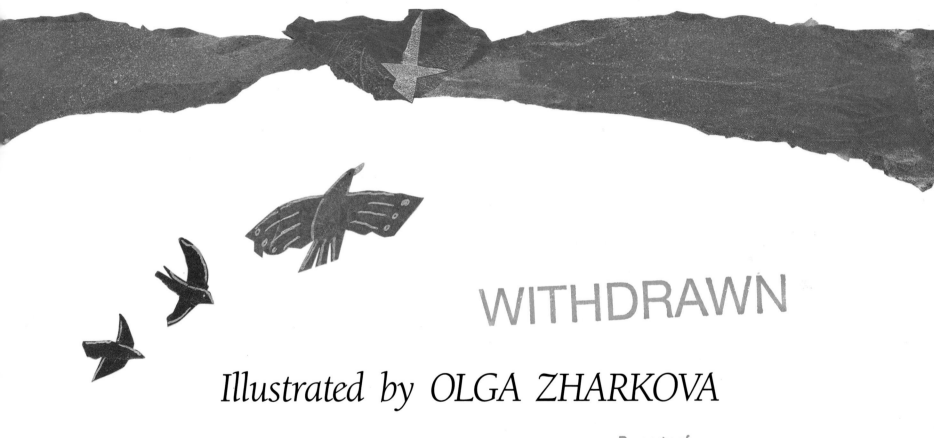

WITHDRAWN

Illustrated by OLGA ZHARKOVA

Property of
FAUQUIER COUNTY PUBLIC LIBRARY
11 Winchester Street
Warrenton, VA 22186

SCHOLASTIC
HARDCOVER

SCHOLASTIC INC. · NEW YORK

We three kings of Orient are,

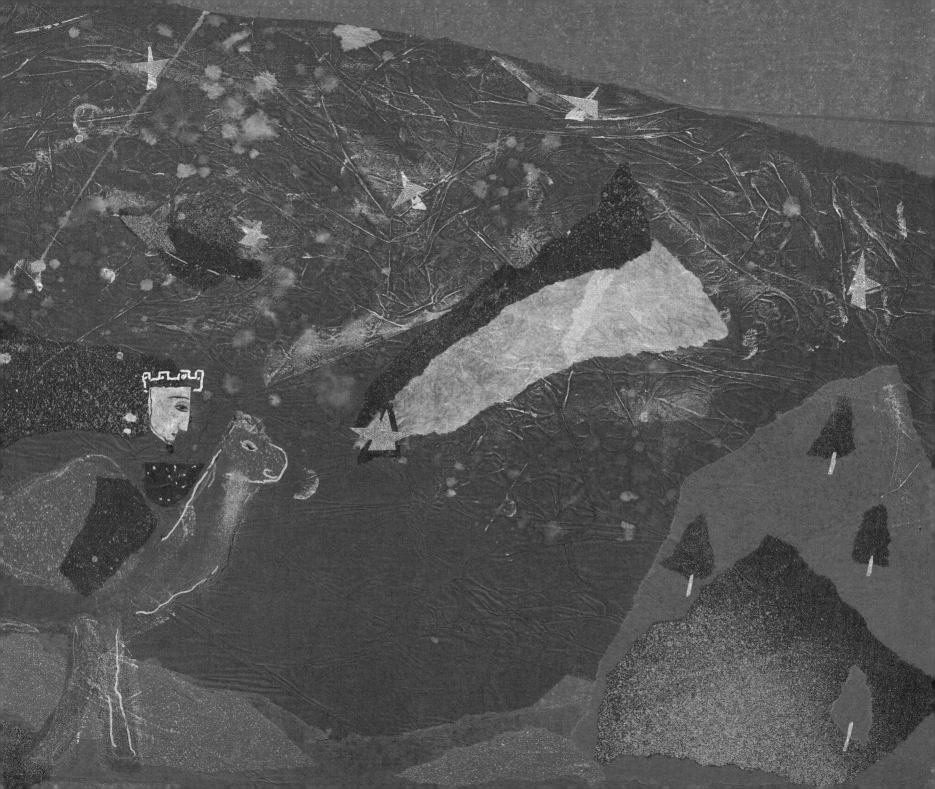

Bearing gifts we traverse afar,
Field and fountain,
Moor and mountain,

Following yonder star.

O star of wonder, star of night,
Star with royal beauty bright;
Westward leading, still proceeding,
Guide us to Thy perfect light.

Born a King on Bethlehem's plain,
Gold I bring to crown Him again,

King forever,
Ceasing never,
Over us all to reign.

O star of wonder, star of night,
Star with royal beauty bright;
Westward leading, still proceeding,
Guide us to Thy perfect light.

Frankincense to offer have I,
Incense owns a Deity nigh,
Prayer and praising,
All men raising,
Worship Him, God on high.

O star of wonder, star of night,
Star with royal beauty bright;
Westward leading, still proceeding,
Guide us to Thy perfect light.

Myrrh is mine; its bitter perfume
Breathes a life of gathering gloom,
Sorrowing, sighing,
Bleeding, dying,
Sealed in the stone-cold tomb.

O star of wonder, star of night,
Star with royal beauty bright;
Westward leading, still proceeding,
Guide us to Thy perfect light.

Glorious now, behold Him arise,
King, and God, and Sacrifice,
Heav'n sings Alleluia:
Alleluia the earth replies.

O star of wonder, star of night,
Star with royal beauty bright;

Westward leading, still proceeding,
Guide us to Thy perfect light.

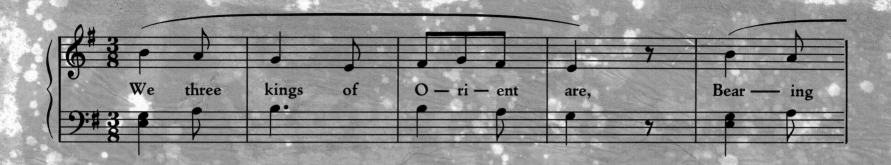

We three kings of O — ri — ent are, Bear — ing

gifts we tra – verse a — far, Field and foun — tain, Moor and

moun — tain, Fol – low – ing yon — der star. O —